The Five Senses

Julie Murray

Abdo
SENSES
Kids

abdopublishing.com

Published by Abdo Kids, a division of ABDO, PO Box 398166, Minneapolis, Minnesota 55439.
Copyright © 2016 by Abdo Consulting Group, Inc. International copyrights reserved in all countries.
No part of this book may be reproduced in any form without written permission from the publisher.

Printed in the United States of America, North Mankato, Minnesota.

052015

092015

 THIS BOOK CONTAINS
RECYCLED MATERIALS

Photo Credits: iStock, Shutterstock

Production Contributors: Teddy Borth, Jennie Forsberg, Grace Hansen

Design Contributors: Candice Keimig, Dorothy Toth

Library of Congress Control Number: 2014958410

Cataloging-in-Publication Data

Murray, Julie.

 The five senses / Julie Murray.

   p. cm. -- (Senses)

ISBN 978-1-62970-924-6

Includes index.

1. Senses and sensation¬--Juvenile literature.   I. Title.

612.8--dc23

                          2014958410

Table of Contents

Senses

We have five senses.

We use them every day!

Our ears hear **sounds**.

This is the sense of hearing.

Our eyes see things.

This is the sense of sight.

Our noses smell things.

This is the sense of smell.

Our mouths taste things.

This is the sense of taste.

Our hands touch things.

This is the sense of touch.

Ben plays basketball.

He feels the ball.

Ben sees his teammates.

He hears the crowd.

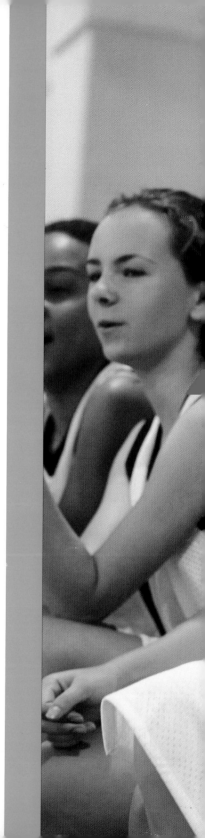

What senses did you use today?

The Five Senses

 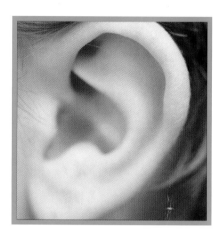

sight   smell   hearing

 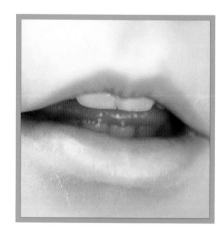

touch   taste

Glossary

crowd
a large number of people in one area, usually for a sports game or other event.

sound
a noise that you can hear.

Index

abdokids.com

Use this code to log on to abdokids.com and access crafts, games, videos, and more!

Abdo Kids Code:
STK9246